mythic blues

june bates
SAPPHIC POETRY

Trigger Warning
Brief mentions of homophobia and sexism.

Other Books By June Bates
she is the poem
the lavender haze

ISBN: 9798399471747

For her.

mythic blues

The way she blushes makes me want to create art.

Yes, you've heard this one before.
Love makes you repeat yourself.
Love makes you tell the same story
over and over again
for years.

I understand Icarus.
I died once, too
trying to kiss
the sun.

BEFORE YOU

I thought love was a dream.

I thought love was a fairytale.

I thought love was enchanting,
but I never thought
it was real.

You make me feel
like I can take on the world.

You make me feel
like sleeping in on Sunday
and having breakfast for dinner
and stealing kisses under covers.
You make me feel
young and stupid and giddy and

—happy

—the word I'm looking for is happy.

Love means
you're comfortable enough
to be vulnerable.

Love means
you're safe.

Now that I understand love,
make me forget.

I want to go back to not knowing.

I hate having something to lose.

-plea to Aphrodite in the middle of the night.

Stealing kisses and getting caught
pretending to be what you're not.

You can't lie to me anymore. I see you.

You can't hide from me anymore. I see you.

I never thought we'd last forever

but I thought we'd have more time than this.

Lost my halo
looking up at her,

but I made her
scream out for god.

Someone always has to win.
And someone has to lose it all.

It isn't always worth the fall.

Stuck with memories and might-have-beens
and closets full of skeletons
who whisper her name in the middle of the night.

It's been a month since she left
and I still can't sleep right.

I am water.
You are thirst.
We are two halves
of the same universe.

You are the ocean
and I am a grain of sand,

tossed in your depths

caught in your current

happy to be lost.

you pick me up from the ashes of heartbreak
and you make me burn brightly again.
I am consumed by your passion
and reborn in your embrace.

-phoenixfire love.

I was told love meant compromise

and dating men always felt like
compromising myself.

-*thought I was doing it right.*

She sings *here comes my man*
and I play vagabond for her.

King me again.
Kiss me where it hurts.

I'll play whatever you want to play.
You don't even have to call me by my name.

It's not fair
that we inherited
such a broken world
but you do make it brighter.
You make life easier.
I always look forward to you.

I hope all of my flaws are forgivable ones.

I hope you can look past the things that I've done.

I loved you. I was brave for you.
Didn't I prove it? Couldn't you see?
Completed heroes tasks on my knees.
Lead your armies.
Died in your arms.

> It was never enough.
> It was never going to be enough.

Call me Orpheus but of course I looked back.
I'm still looking back.
I couldn't go that long without my eyes on you.
Forgive me.

I've known Artemis intimately.
They say she ran with the wolves
but she ran with me.
We hid in the mountains.
We hid across the sea.
We considered changing our names.
Anything to be free.

-Callisto

You were
the most
important thing
in my life.

Now you're gone
and I'm just left
with my life.

I thought we were The Lovers
but you shot me through the heart.

Even your leaving looked like art.

I thought you were Queen of Cups,
now your swords are in my side.

I'm taking it in stride.

I knew how this would end

before we even touched
before we even kissed.

-oracle & prophesy.

I miss
the way my room
used to always
smell like you.

I'll be fine.

It just takes time to unbecome.
That's what you have to do when love leaves.
Separate yourself from the wreckage.
Find pieces worth saving.

Forgive me my tenderness.
Forgive me my weakness.
Even after the last time and the last,
after the end times,
after I kicked every other lover out of my bed
out of my head, out of my heart—

I left room for you.

There's still a light on
if you want to come home.

If I were a king,
I'd send my knights to guard your castle.
But I'm just half a man
and too much of a hassle.

It don't make you the asshole if you leave.

You're still everything to me.

If not a tale as old as time,
a tale as old as lesbians,

we were just friends

(Good friends, best friends.)

and nothing more.

Until we closed the curtains
and we locked the doors,
fell in love in my apartment
on the second floor.
You slept there so often
that you called it yours.

(You called me yours.)

When I told my mother about you,
she didn't know what to say, so
she talked about the past
and the life she thought I'd have.

Some parents mourn the day their children start thinking for themselves and speaking up and making their own choices.

I love you so much
that if one of us died
I'd petition the stars
to put your face in the sky.

-*we'd make new constellations.*

Everything I've ever written
has been queer.

Even before I knew.
Even before I understood.
Everything I've ever touched
has love's fingerprints on it.

I contemplated the coward's way out

but I'd rather be proud.

There are things I still can't say,
not even in the poetry.

I still want to be that girl who forgives
but I am a woman who has learned hard truths.

I mistook coincidence for fate / she was just a girl / she was just a person close enough to touch.

My heart is a glue trap / it doesn't matter if love deserves to die in me / it always does.

Maybe in the future when we're better, stronger people I'll walk up to her and not feel my heart cracking in half.

You can burn us and ban us
and bar us from public life

but history has already tried
your big ideas.

and queers rise.

PRAYING

I'm trying
to be brave
but I don't want to
have to fight.

> *No one*
> *wants to fight*
> *for their life, June.*

> *What other option is there?*

We must practice kindness radically
—not niceness, not falsity
—true kindness.

We must also know that kindness
will not stop the blood or the bullets.

They want us to hide.
To cower.
To slink back into the shadows.
I will not live in life's closet.
I refuse to only see the sun through the blinds.

I will not stand here on my pulpit
debating our right to live freely and love openly.

Words are not enough.

That's why we threw bricks.

-June 28, 1969

All the people I loved before were practice for something real. I barely noticed being left or leaving—and then there was you, sucking all the air out of the room, taking the sun with you, burning the house down on your way out of town.

I've climbed out of the mouth of hell before.
I can do it again.

I'm sorry. I don't know what else to say.
We should have run away, like you said.
I should have given everything up for you.

Forgive me for my wishful thinking.

Forgive me for rewriting the past
until it's easy to stomach.

Whenever I'm awake
in the middle of the night

I'm always thinking about you.

I wish you'd just
show up on my doorstep again
bewitching me
with green eyes
and sweet words,
all of your delicious poison.

-it's over for you, but it's not over for me.

You kissed me
and my fears didn't evaporate.
They doubled.
I started counting down the days
until you'd disappear.
No one has ever
been brave enough
to stay.

I was dancing with him

but I was watching her
all night long.

Sorry I can't stick to one muse.
I have too much to say.
Love is too big in my life
to live any other way.

Can't wait for July.
My heart needs a holiday.
I need to run away again.
Let me hang my head
somewhere she never
put her hands on me.

I know it's over,
but the art doesn't.

My pen still weeps your name
across the page.

I set my life
on fire
for the chance

to touch her

and now I must
deal with the wreckage.

these days
when I think of you

I cry
instead of
writing

so

that's kind of how it's going

Why did you bother
saving my life

if you were just
going to ruin it later?

I can't be mad that it didn't work out. I just can't be.
You still changed my life. You still pulled me out of
the dark and wrapped rainbows around my heart.
You still brought the light in.

My parents tell me
Pride is a sin
and I

stop fighting them.

"Fine. And?"

So many people misunderstand Pride.
Publicly identifying yourself as queer.
Being loud and colorful and open.

I don't do it for you.
I don't even do it for me.
I do it for the girl I used to be
and for others like her.

Seeing happy queer people
living openly
is what lured me out of the closet.

Our community
will always
be stronger together.

Infighting
when our rights are at stake
is like a snake
biting its own tail.

Why are we
eating ourselves alive

when there are those cheer on,

wishing and hoping and
praying to see us dead?

Queerness has opened up the world for me
and given it new meaning.

Thank you for making me brave.

Sometimes I hate who I am
but I still have to live with her

so I try to make peace.

I should have called the day you left.
Now I sleep with my regrets.

I should have done more than call.

I should have run down the street
screaming your name
right in front of everyone.

One day,
something will snap into place
and finally make me give up on us.

I hope it never comes.
I hope it comes tomorrow.

I wrote all of this for you.
I know it isn't enough.

I have to believe
that I can move on
and fall out of love with you

and still be your friend.

Can't the aftermath of love
be clean and easy just this once?

You weren't my first love,
but you were my first forever.

STAR-CROSSED

Some things were never
meant to last.

You can fight your fate

but you have to fight it forever.

We both deserved easier love stories
and more dependable lovers.

I played the memories on repeat
for too long. Remembering you
felt good even when it hurt me.

OLD HABITS

I still lived on our love even after it died.
Quitting is hard.

I hope you don't blame me.

Pomegranate Dream

a sapphic retelling
of the Hades & Persephone myth

There was only darkness
before she brought the light.

Persephone:
gorgeous Goddess of Spring

Hades:
miserable King of the Underworld

You know the story.
Daisies bloom wherever she steps.
Everything is gold and green in her wake.

And I am a Ruiner of Good Things.

She raised flowers from barren earth.
She thawed my heart like spring.

BREAKING NEWS IN HELL

Prince of Heartache and Darkness,
King of all the devils and mad revelers,
Hades

is in love.

(And it's bad for optics.)

(Looks weak.)

What do you want?
What can I do?
What sacrifice must I make
to be worthy of your presence
right here
in my life
forever?

Tell me what it takes, Persephone.

I'll do anything.

I'm already on my knees.

She demanded my heart
so I cut it right out of my chest.

She said, "No. Not like that.
Here.
Let me show you."

And then she kissed me
so hard
I saw constellations.

I always thought
love would make you stronger.
Now that I have it,
I just know it makes you vulnerable.

-strength and weakness.

THE ROMEO AND JULIET OF IT ALL

Loving each other should be easy
but it's not.

So we kiss in cars and behind closed doors.
We keep our love safe in secret.

I show my heart
and everyone recoils

but her.

I know I'm not good enough for you.
I never will be.
You deserve more than this life has to offer.

~~But, please~~

When she touches me,
my entire body turns into a garden.
Spring blossoms everywhere
her hands land.

I never thought anyone
would understand me
the way you understand me.

But now that you know me,
you can destroy me.

That's the price we pay for love.

I came out of hiding for her.
She made me love the sun.

I won't lie.
In the beginning,
there was something about the risk
that made everything thrilling.

Her eyes on mine in a crowd.
Sneaking touches when no one was looking.
Finding places to hide.

But love is supposed to be comfortable
and easy.

I didn't want us
looking over our shoulders
forever.

I wanted to be free.

"Baby," I said. "Maybe it's time
you tell your mother about us.
Maybe it's time we get serious.
Maybe—"

She kissed me before I could finish.

NEXT WEEK, SHE MOVED IN

"What kind of king lives in an apartment?"
Persephone laughed.

"Best view in Hell," I said. "You can
have your own wing and there's still space.
It's bigger than it looks."

She put down the box in her hands and wrapped her
arms around me. "I don't ever want to be far away
from you again," she said.

We moved her things into my room that night.

Hell tastes like heaven when she's around.
Before her, I was lost and now I am found.
When the room spins, she's my ground.

And then the thunder boomed
and the mountain fell down.
Persephone's mother was sniffing around.
Didn't like what her daughter
was doing downtown.

"The family name" and all.

Demeter ordered her daughter home,
said I don't like the way you've grown
said I don't want you on his throne
said you are better off alone.

Persephone said no.

BREAKING NEWS ON MOUNT OLYMPUS

Our darling Persephone has been stolen away.
Taken advantage of. Tempted by sin.

Help us get Persephone home to her mother!
Demand justice!

And sign this petition to banish Hades
and his people permanently to the Underworld.

Together, we can keep our children safe.

I lay awake at night next to her,
marveling over the fact that
no one outside of this room
really knows me.

I can't stomach
half the things
they say about me.

I want to respond to the news but
Persephone tells me to calm down.

She sighs,
and says she misses her mother
and she misses the meadow

and she loves me

but she hates hiding in the dark.

They talk about pomegranates
and devil's tricks
and liar's tongues

but it was
just a promise.

I said, I know it's complicated.

I know you're more flower than moon.
You don't shine at midnight like I do.
Darkness has been unkind to you.
You want to be free,
out there.

So, go (if you need to)

run as far as you need to.
Revisit your old life
or make a new one.

But if you ever need some shade,
please

come home.

The next day,
she was gone.

AND NOW

the months do roll on.

I'm always sure I just missed her call.

I lay awake at night
missing the sound of her breathing.

I burn when her eyes aren't on mine.

I don't exist
when she's not looking right at me.

I KNOW IT'S WEAK

I'm still waiting for her to come home.

US

I can't close this book.
The story isn't over.

There are still things I need to say.

Thank you for reading! Please review if you can spare a minute. I appreciate you so much. Thank you for taking a chance on my words.

About the Author

June Bates is the behind the collections *She Is The Poem* and *The Lavender Haze.* She hopes to have more to say here one day.

She reads every single one of your emails.
junebatespoet@gmail.com

Printed in Great Britain
by Amazon

35865653R00067